Camping

The Ultimate Guide to Getting Started On Your First Camping Trip

Beth McRoberts

Table of Contents

Preface

Never been camping? You're in for a treat. There is something about sleeping outdoors and spending your days surrounded by nature that makes the human mind relax.

To the beginner, planning a camping trip that will go smoothly can seem daunting. Don't worry, it's easier than it looks! You'll quickly get a feel for what is needed when sleeping outdoors, but to ensure that your first trip goes well, this book will give you all the hints and tips you need.

There are a few types of camping. For this first trip, we'll be looking at the first option, Campsite Camping.

Campsite Camping

Setting up your tent in an organized campground is definitely the way to go for your first night out. You'll be far more comfortable and can ease into the experience, as opposed to wild camping. You will have access to a few amenities while still enjoying the outdoor experience.

Glamping

Glamping is essentially luxury camping and usually involves oversized tents or even trailers and all the comforts of home. Electronics and cooking gear are brought along. Some people even have entire outdoor kitchens! This type of camping is definitely not roughing it.

Wild Camping

Do you enjoy shows like Survivorman? While you probably won't be eating grubs to stay alive, this type of camping is certainly more basic than the other two types. You will be hiking to find the perfect camping spot, clearing your own space and setting up a shelter or even building your own. There are no cushy toilets or fresh running water out in the middle of nowhere and you'll be carrying everything in on your back.

While all of these are valid camping choices, most people do best with a nice campground to start out in. It gets your outdoor life off to a good start and lets you experience the best of camping.

7 Secrets to an Awesome First Camping Trip

For your first trip, it's a good idea to head to a local campground. There's nothing worse than driving all day and arriving after dark at a new place and having to hike your gear into the woods to find a good camping spot. Once you have more experience, you will want to venture further abroad, but your first trip should be to an established campground or nearby national park.

When choosing a place to stay, there are a few things you should consider. These are my seven secrets to the perfect camping location.

1. Pick an Established Campground

Why? Well, you'll appreciate not having to deal with leveling the forest floor before setting up your tent, for one, and you will also enjoy having bathroom facilities in the vicinity. While these will be considerably more rustic than you are used to, it certainly beats digging your own holes in the forest.

2. Get Recommendations

One of the best ways to find the perfect camping spot is to just ask your friends. Make sure they know that you want a place that is good for beginners.

If your friends are like you and have yet to embark on their first outdoor adventure, you'll want to look online for recommendations.

3. Book Ahead

Summer is a popular time to go camping, so you're going to run into some competition for spots. The simplest way to resolve this is to call the campground nice and early in the season and book your preferred dates. Remember that it's best to enjoy the warmer months, since winter camping is a whole different ball game.

4. Make the First Campout a Short One

One or two nights is a good way to start. It is far simpler to plan for a short trip than it is to come up with everything you need for a full week in the bush. Longer trips can be a lot of fun, but you can whet your appetite with a weekend away.

This is also a trial run. No matter how prepared you are, there will be things that you've missed or that you didn't need, but carried to the campsite anyway. Each camping trip will hone your packing skills and help you realize what is truly necessary.

5. Don't Take Too Much

It's tempting to pack everything you possibly can in order to ensure success, but you'll just end up with too much. Remember that most campsites don't have parking right in front of the tent and all that equipment will have to be hauled to your tent. Even if you are parking next to the campsite, there is no need to overload your vehicle with "stuff."

6. Pitch Your Camp in Daylight

Tents can be challenging enough to set up when you can actually see what you're doing, but they are a nightmare in the dark. Make sure you leave yourself plenty of time to get your camp set up long before the sun goes down. It's a good idea to check what time the sun sets since most people aren't familiar with the exact time.

If you're camping a few hours from home, leave nice and early to give yourself time for any issues that might come up.

7. Bring Extra Batteries

Flashlights have the annoying tendency to die just when you need them the most and it is almost always because the batteries have died. Make sure to pack extras or choose a flashlight that can be hand pumped to recharge it. There are also flashlights and lanterns that have handles you can turn to charge the battery.

Your first trip out is all about trial and error, but you can save yourself a lot of hassle if you follow these secrets to success.

Gearing Up: What You Need

Take a look at any camping gear catalog or website and you'll instantly be convinced you need to spend thousands just to get the basics. Nothing could be further from the truth. Some things are worth paying more for, of course, but other items don't need to be name brand or even brand new.

There are also levels of luxury while camping. We'll start with the basics and move up to the more luxury items later on.

What You Absolutely Need for Camping

Tent: A tent is essential if you are going to stay out of the elements and keep yourself protected during the night. Tents can be used, but you will want to make sure that they are leak proof.

A tent should be large enough to hold everyone in your party (alternatively, you can use more than one tent), but not too big. Large tents are a pain to set up and can be difficult to heat with just body heat. Keep in mind that most tents are labeled with how many people will fit, but if you are medium to large sized, you will probably want a little extra space to maneuver in.

Ground Tarp: A tarp doesn't have to be anything fancy and can be used. Its main purpose is to protect the bottom of the tent from sharp objects and to give an extra layer against moisture and cold. Keep the tarp tucked under the tent to avoid rain running under there.

Claw hammer: A hammer will help you pound in the tent stakes and pull out the stakes when you go.

Sleeping Bag: Your sleeping bag doesn't have to be name brand or super expensive, but it should be rated for the climate you'll be sleeping in. Look for a bag that is rated for the lowest temperature you will be camping out in.

Sleep Pad: Stay nice and comfy with a sleeping pad or mattress. Cold ground can wick your body heat away and you'll wake up freezing in the middle of the night. Lay down a foam pad or an inflatable mattress to avoid this common issue. If nothing else, you can always spread out a blanket to help cushion you from the ground.

Lantern/Flashlight: It gets very, very dark away from streetlights. While many established campgrounds have some form of lighting, most areas will be far darker than you are used to. Have a light to help you find your way to the bathroom or tent in the night.

Flashlights are a standard on a camping trip, but you will probably find a headlamp even more practical since it leaves your hands free. A lantern can also be hung in a tree or from a hook in the tent to cast hands free lighting.

Insect Repellent: Don't get eaten alive! Summer is a great time for camping and it's also a great time for bugs. Cover any exposed skin to prevent long nights of itching.

Water bottles: Carrying fresh water on hikes is essential, so make sure you have a way to take some with you. Water bottles with built in filters can be handy if you plan to drink from lakes and rivers, but for pure water, any bottle will do.

Bucket: A bucket can be used for everything from rinsing food to carrying water in. It's a good idea to keep a bucket of water near the fire, as well.

Food and Water: We'll get into this more in the next chapter, but it's always a good idea to keep some nourishment on you. If you want to be a little fancier, take along some adult beverages for the grown-ups, like beer and wine.

Matches: You can't start a fire easily without a box of matches, so don't forget these!

Tinfoil: Even if you don't have a pot to cook in, tinfoil can be used to wrap food for roasting or even to make one-time use containers for heating leftovers.

Knife: A good knife is essential around the campsite. You'll use it for everything from whittling points on your roasting sticks to chopping up the freshly caught fish for dinner.

Rope: This is one of those things that is always handy. Rope can be used to string up a tarp, to tie sticks together to make a teepee for the kids, or to create a clothesline to dry clothing and sleeping bags.

Duct Tape: You should always have duct tape with you, whether you're camping or not. It has hundreds of uses, including taping up wounds, patching leaks in the tent and holding things together.

Toilet Paper: Leaves just don't cut it. Enough said. Bring your own rolls of toilet paper and some plastic bags to keep the garbage in if you are doing your business in the woods.

Soap: Staying clean is a necessity when you are at a campground. You'll be amazed at how fast hands and faces get dirty.

Taking Your Camping Up a Notch

Not so interested in camping at the basic level? Here's what you'll need to enjoy the outdoors a little more.

Welcome Mat: Tents have the tendency to collect dirt and dust, so a small mat outside the door to wipe feet on can help keep the debris down. You don't need anything special, just bring along the mat from home.

Saw: Fallen branches and trees are rarely the ideal size for a campfire and a saw makes it easier to cut them into manageable pieces. You can also bring an axe if you are comfortable chopping wood.

Extra tarp: If you end up in the rain, it's helpful to have an extra tarp to string up over your sitting area, so you don't have to spend the whole time in the tent.

Air Pump: Planning on using an inflatable mattress or other air filled item? While you can fill it with air from your mouth, a pump is infinitely easier. Don't forget to bring a patch kit, too, in case your inflatables spring a leak.

Pots and Pans: Leave your favorite pots and pans at home. They will be blackened with the first meal over an open fire. If you are using a camp stove, you can use regular pans. Otherwise, check the thrift store to see if they have any cheap pots that you can use without worry over coals.

Camp Stove: Whether there is a fire ban or not, a camp stove can be handy to have around. You don't have to wait for the fire to burn down and for those who are not accustomed to cooking over an open fire, it can be challenging. A camp stove functions just like a gas stove, so it is relatively easy to use.

Everyone will have their own must-have items they just can't live without. These are usually luxuries, so consider this if you have to haul everything in to the campsite! There's no point in making five trips between the car and the distant campsite if you don't really need everything you're taking.

After the first few camping trips, you will become an expert at packing light and paring down the weight to make your journey easier. All it really takes is one long hike with too much weight for you to realize exactly what you really need.

Eats and Treats: Packing Food

As wonderful as it is to be in the great outdoors, chances are it will give you an appetite. There's something about the fresh air and exercise that makes people hungry, so you'll want to plan ahead for the increased food intake.

Food Safety

When you think of food safety, what comes to mind? If you're considering camping, it's probably protecting your food from wild animals like bears. At home, you probably worry more about whether or not the food you have prepared is good or not. We'll look at both of these issues, but in this section, we're going to focus on preparing and keeping food safely to avoid getting sick.

You might want to cook up some steaks or hot dogs while you have the campfire going. While this is a delicious way to celebrate your first camping trip, you'll want to avoid any bacterial issues.

Meat cannot be left out at room temperature for long before it begins to spoil. Keeping your steaks in a cooler will help, but only until the ice melts, so you should plan to eat any meat your first night at the campground.

Other foods that should be treated with care include:

Seafood

Poultry

Lunch meats

Mayonnaise (if it contains eggs)

Salad dressing (if it contains eggs)

All of these foods should be left at home or eaten from a cooler on the first day. Anything left once the cooler ice is melted needs to be thrown away.

The Best Camping Foods

What should you take on your camping adventure, besides hot dogs for the first night? That really depends on whether or not you want to spend much time cooking.

It's a good idea to have some ready-to-eat snacks that you can grab when hunger attacks. You probably won't want to cook all day, so plan to have some items like granola bars, apples or chips to munch on between meals.

You can't go wrong with sandwiches either, even if they are just good old peanut butter and jelly. Look for shelf-stable mayonnaise or vegan mayonnaise to use as a spread for veggie sandwiches like tomatoes or cucumbers, which will keep just fine for a few days in a cool place.

Easy Campfire Meals

The simplest meals to prepare don't involve a pot or a pan, just the fire and maybe a stick or some tinfoil. You can make some pretty amazing meals this way.

While sausages and marshmallows are an obvious thing to cook on a stick, you can actually make quite a few dishes with just a stick.

Bannock: This is also referred to as campfire bread. While extremely simple, this is a meal in itself and even better with honey drizzled over it.

To make bannock, mix 1 cup of flour, 1 teaspoon of baking powder, ¼ teaspoon of salt and 2 tablespoons of powdered milk in a zipper bag or small container. Add a tablespoon of oil when you're ready to make it and gradually add water until you have thick dough. This can all be mixed in the bag. Let the mixture sit for five minutes.

Wrap the dough around a green stick, making sure it's no thicker than about half an inch at any point so it will cook well. Turn the stick slowly over the coals until the bannock is darkened and slides easily off the stick.

Baked Potatoes: Poke holes in some large potatoes and wrap them tightly in foil. Toss the potatoes in the hot coals, turning once in a while. It takes around 30 minutes to cook potatoes this way. Test with a fork before you open the package to make sure it's done. Then smother the potato in margarine and dried bacon bits for a delicious, simple meal.

Toasted bread and cheese: Toast tastes amazing when cooked over an open fire. Use a toast fork or a forked stick to gently toast the bread over the fire. Flip the bread once one side is toasted and sprinkle with grated cheese. Continue to cook until the bottom is toasted to perfection and the cheese is melted.

Campfire Burritos: Grab a tin of refried beans, a little grated cheese, some onions and tomatoes and a few tortillas and you have the makings of a tasty breakfast. Spread the beans on a tortilla, top with cheese, minced onions and tomatoes and roll up. Wrap in tinfoil and cook over the coals for 10-15 minutes or until the cheese melts.

Tinfoil Popcorn: Place two tablespoons of popcorn kernels in the middle of a large (18 inch) piece of heavy duty tinfoil. Pour two tablespoons of oil over the kernels and carefully fold the edges together, sealing tightly, to make a large pouch. Use wire to attach the packet to a stick and then shake gently over the fire until the kernels stop popping. Salt and serve.

Baked Bananas: Slice the peel of a banana down the middle and open slightly. Sprinkle cinnamon and sugar inside and wrap the banana tightly in tinfoil. Bake in the coals for 15-20 minutes or until cooked through.

Gourmet Campsite Meals

Looking for something to impress your friends and family? There are plenty of things you can do with minimal materials!

Chili: Bring along a few cans of pre-made chili or make your own. Tinned tomatoes, beans and some freshly chopped onions are all you need for a very basic chili, but you can add canned or dried meat and any other ingredients you want. Just dump it all in a pot and simmer over the coals for an hour or so to heat it up and let the flavors meld.

Toad in the Hole: This classic recipe requires nothing more than a slice of bread and an egg. Tear the center of the bread out and place the slice in a greased frying pan. Crack the egg into the hole and cook until the egg starts to set. Flip the bread and egg over and cook through. You can add sliced tomatoes or grated cheese if you like.

Pasta: Boiling water is pretty basic, so if you have a pot, you can make pasta. Add a packaged sauce or just chop some onions and tomatoes to add to the pasta after draining, along with a little olive oil. There are plenty of packaged specialty dishes, too, like shells and cheese or alfredo sauce. You'll probably want to have some powdered milk with you for these.

Roasted Apples: Push a stick through a peeled apple and turn slowly over the fire until soft and cooked through. Sprinkle with cinnamon and sugar before eating.

Instant Oatmeal: Buy these or make your own with 1/3 cup quick oats, 1 teaspoon powdered milk, a pinch of salt, 2 teaspoons of sugar and a dash of cinnamon. Keep the mixture in a zipper bag and just add 2/3 cup of boiling water to each packet of mix and stir well. Let it sit for a couple of minutes before eating.

Pancakes: Yes, you can have pancakes while you're on a camping trip! Mix 1.5 cups of flour, 1 tablespoon of sugar, a dash of salt and 3 teaspoons of baking powder in a zipper bag before you leave home. At the campsite, heat the pan and mix 1 egg, 3 tablespoons of oil and 1-1.5 cups milk until the mixture is as thick as you want. Cook like you normally would, in a frying pan, over the fire or cook stove.

Don't Forget the Drinks!

While water is the best way to stay hydrated, you'll probably want to indulge your taste buds from time to time. Adults might enjoy a cold beer, kept cold by submerging in the ocean or river. Kids will be thrilled to have juice boxes or even drink mixes to add to purified water.

Powdered drink mixes can hide the taste of water that has been treated to make it safe, so you should always have some along. Tea and coffee are also handy beverages to keep around.

Purifying water is as simple as using a hand pumped filter or a gravity filter. However, if you don't have either of these, boiling the water for ten minutes will kill anything in it, but also makes it taste flat. Iodine or bleach can also purify water and make it safe to drink.

Most campers prefer to bring their own bottled water on their first trip if there is nothing available at the park they are planning to visit. Some campsites provide pure water from taps or pumps set around the park.

Comfort in the Wild

Think camping is uncomfortable? Don't worry, it doesn't have to be!
There are a few things you should know about staying comfy while you're
out in the woods.

Clear the Tent Site

Before you set up camp, rake or sweep the area where the tent will go. Get
rid of any rocks or twigs that are scattered around. They might look small,
but they'll feel like boulders when you're lying on top of one in the night!

Wear Layers

Outside of the air conditioned offices and heated homes, the weather can
change drastically. You might be stifling hot after a long walk to the
campsite, but freezing once the sun goes down. The trick is to wear layers.
Bring a t-shirt, a long sleeved shirt and a sweater to stay warm at night.
You can also keep a hat nearby, to prevent heat from escaping out your
head.

Air Everything Out

Tents and sleeping bags can smell pretty musty if it is damp. Bring along some rope and make your own clothesline. Air out the sleeping bags, clothes and other items and leave the tent open for a few hours during the least buggy part of the day to help things dry out. You'll also want to move most things out of the tent to prevent moisture from being trapped under it.

A little air freshener can also make the whole place smell better if things are getting musty or if stinky feet are taking over.

Bring a Chair

Camping chairs can save your life! Well, not really, but they will save your butt from going numb after sitting on a log for hours on end. Most camping chairs are folding and take up very little space, so you can toss one in the car. If you are hiking to your location, you might not want to take everything with you, but there are very lightweight folding stools on the market, too.

Tent Alternatives

If you prefer to skip the tent and you're camping on your own, why not try a hammock? Just string it up between a couple of trees and you're good to go. You will want a blanket or two underneath you, though, to keep the cold air from sapping your body heat.

There are even hammocks available that are completely enclosed, so you can stay secure and away from bugs. Even if you choose not to sleep in a hammock, having one in your campsite is nice for resting up and relaxing.

It's the Little Things

Sometimes it's just the little details that make the difference between being miserable and thoroughly enjoying your camping trip. Consider what makes your day before you pack up and head out and try to incorporate that into your adventure.

Can't deal without your morning coffee or cup of tea? Bring along a kettle and make sure you get your caffeine fix first thing in the morning. You can even use a French press to brew some of the best coffee around.

Does music keep you going? Bring a handcrank or solar radio or just a few extra batteries for an mp3 player.

Another trick is to bring extra socks so you can change as needed. There's nothing better than a nice dry pair of socks to make you feel like everything is going to be just fine.

Fun in the Sun: Awesome Camping Activities

Hey, you've made it and you're all set up. You're actually camping! It might even be getting a little bit boring. So now what?

The following activities will keep you and your friends or family busy and happy while you're all out in the woods.

Take a Hike

Take full advantage of being in the wilderness and enjoy nature with a long hike. If you are staying in a national park, this will be especially rewarding. Grab a map on your way in so you can find the best spots to check out.

Cool Off with Swimming

Wading and splashing in a lake or calm river is often the highlight of a camping trip. The entire family can enjoy swimming and it's a great way to cool off after you've taken a long hike.

Try Stargazing

The night sky is amazing in the countryside, away from the light pollution of town. If you miss this opportunity to step away from the fire and stare up at the stars, you'll be missing one of the most incredible experiences available to you. Spread out a blanket and lie on your back with a friend. See how many constellations you can spot.

Improve Your Photography Skill

There's no shortage of photography subjects when you're camping. From wildlife and flowers to your children and sunsets, this is the perfect time to snap some shots that will go straight into the family album. Just don't get so caught up in taking photos that you miss out on actually having fun!

Get Your Frisbee Game On

Ultimate Frisbee or just regular Frisbee can be a fun way to spend an afternoon, particularly if there are others who would enjoy playing. This can be an activity that brings in other campers and helps you make new friends. Bring a few extras along, since they do tend to get lost in the trees sometimes.

Play a Board Game

While it might not seem like the first choice of activities, board games break up the monotony around camp when nothing else appeals. If it's raining out, you can also spend those damp hours playing an epic game of Monopoly with a friend.

Search for Treasure

Geocaching is a fun hobby that you may be able to do where you plan to camp. Check online to find out if there are any caches in the area, break out the GPS and start hunting down that treasure!

Tell Ghost Stories

What kind of camping trip would it be without ghost stories around the campfire? Just make sure you keep it tame if there are children around . . . you can tell the really spooky tales once the little ones are in bed.

Try Your Hand at Fishing

Not all lakes permit fishing and you may need special permission, so check before taking along all your gear. Fishing can be very relaxing and for many, there is nothing like frying up a fresh trout for dinner before turning in to bed.

Get Creative with Bushcraft

Creating items from found materials is a great way to spend some time in your camp. You can weave a basket from reeds or create your own bow and arrow from sticks. Kids can really get into this part of camping.

One tip is to use only what you find on the ground. Don't start hacking down branches to build a chair that you'll only use for one day. Look for fallen branches and use those instead.

Break Out the Musical Instruments

Strumming on a guitar in the middle of the woods is almost a religious experience. It just feels right. You don't need a lot of fancy instruments, but if anyone in your group plays, try jamming together. Anyone who doesn't play can drum with sticks or sing.

There's plenty of fun to be had around a campsite. If you have a favorite outdoor sport, bring along the equipment you need to play it. You might even find a new hobby in this list.

Staying Healthy: First Aid Tips and Tricks

You are more likely to be injured when you are camping, simply because you'll be doing more than sitting in front of a television set. The uneven terrain, open fire and water and bugs can all contribute to a higher injury rate. As long as you're careful, you probably won't need more than a bandage now and then. Accidents do happen, though, so being prepared is a good thing.

For your first camping trip, you shouldn't be too far from help, but having a good first aid kit on hand is a necessity. You'll want one with all the basics, including:

Gloves

Bandages in assorted sizes

Gauze and medical tape

Scissors

Elastic bandage

Antiseptic cream

Pain relievers

Tweezers

Calamine lotion

Antiseptic towelettes

Alcohol gel

Allergy medications

If the kit you purchase doesn't have everything you need, you can always add to it. Some people like to include things like chemical cold or heat packs, or numbing spray. You can pack anything you deem necessary.

It's also handy to have a first aid book of procedures. This can be printed off or it may come with the kit. Even if you are well-versed in first aid, you might have difficulty remembering the techniques when someone you love is injured.

The most common first aid issues are:

Allergies: Anyone with allergies will probably have a flare up during a camping trip. All that nature can be a bad thing if your body isn't up for it. Taking allergy medication can help you enjoy the trip.

Bug Bites: Avoid bug bites by wearing long sleeves and pants tucked into socks or using bug spray. You should also make sure the tent remains zipped when the bugs are around. If you or your kids are bitten by mosquitoes, applying calamine can help.

Watch out for ticks when camping, too. These bugs can cause several diseases, including Lyme disease. Check everyone for ticks at the end of the day and remove them with tweezers. If a bulls-eye rash appears within a week or two of the bite, head to the doctor, since this is a sign of Lyme disease.

Burns: Cooking over an open fire is fun, but it also puts you at higher risk for being burned. Burns should be rinsed with cool water and a burn bandage may be applied. For burns that are larger than the palm of your hand or white or charred looking, head to the nearest ER immediately.

Poison ivy/oak: Everyone in the group should know which plants to avoid, but if they do end up with a rash, scrub the area with soap and water and change the person's clothes immediately. Calamine lotion can help ease the itchiness. Benadryl can also help.

Sprains: Hiking can result in a twisted ankle or even a sprain. These are first aid situations that can usually be handled in camp, but if you feel the sprain is severe or there may be a break, head to the hospital. For minor injuries, soak the ankle (or wrist) in cold water and wrap with an elastic bandage for support. Avoid using the joint too much.

Cuts and small wounds: It's pretty common to end up with cuts and scratches while you are out in the woods. These shouldn't cause any problems for the most part, but it's always a good idea to keep things clean. You can also apply antiseptic and a bandage to keep dirt out of open wounds.

Splinters: Small bits of wood may end up in your skin when handling wood on a regular basis. You can use tweezers or a clean needle to remove the splinter. If it doesn't come out, put a bandage over it and try again later. Often the body will expel the piece on its own.

Sunburn: Wear sunscreen to prevent a burn. If you do end up with a sunburn, calamine or aloe vera gel can help reduce the pain and inflammation, as can over the counter anti-inflammatories.

Stay Sane While Camping with Kids

When you announce that you are going camping with your children, the first reaction you'll hear is, "are you crazy?" Maybe you are, but there are ways to preserve your sanity while out in the woods.

Establish Rules Before You Go

Make a list of rules to follow before you go on your camping trip. These might include things like:

"Stay away from the fire unless an adult is there to supervise."

"No throwing sticks or rocks in the campground."

"Always let someone know where you're going," or "Don't go anywhere alone, always take a sibling or parent."

These are rules to be established for safety, of course, so keep them brief and to the point. The types of rules will depend on the ages of your children

Before you head out, sit everyone down and go over the rules with them. When you arrive at the campground, make sure they remember everything and reinforce the rules by providing a fitting consequence if they break a rule. For example, if a child stirs the fire when he's not supposed to be near it, he might not be permitted to cook his own s'more's in the evening.

You aren't the only one with rules, though! Read through the campground rules with the family before setting up your camp and make sure everything is understood.

Plan Your Campsite Carefully

While everyone has to figure out where to put the tent and campfire, etc. planning this layout with kids is a bit more complex. The fire will need to be off to one side and the drink cooler set out of the way to prevent kids from running into the fire or a hot camp stove, etc. Look at where each part of the campsite is and figure out where your kids will be running as they move from place to place. This can help avoid accidents.

Buy some brightly colored flagging tape and mark things like the tent pegs or guide wires to keep kids (and grownups!) from tripping over them.

Keep Them Busy

Bored children tend to fight and bug each other. The best way to avoid the camping trip turning into one big disaster is to ensure that the kids have something to do at all times. And that doesn't mean handing them portable video games!

Give every member of the family a job they need to do. Depending on their ages, children may pick up garbage around camp, wash the dishes after dinner, collect dry wood, watch younger siblings or even take on the responsibility of making cold snacks and meals.

This is a great time to engage with your children. Take them on hikes and track animals, play ball with them or tell each other spooky stories. Show them how to skip rocks or build a mini lean-to to play in.

You can also create an obstacle course or have kids do a scavenger hunt, looking for different nature items. Bring a plastic tub of toys for them to play with in the dirt or sand and toss in a few bottles of dollar store bubbles.

If your children are used to having computers and television, it might take a bit of time for them to get into playing and exploring outdoors. Once they do, however, good luck trying to get them home again!

Feed Them Often

Kids can turn into little brats when they're hungry. When they are running around the woods and climbing trees, you can expect their usual appetite to increase drastically. Plan accordingly and bring lots of extra snacks. You might want to plan for larger meals, as well.

Remember that finger foods are your friend in the woods. Who wants to wash dishes constantly with no hot, running water? Not Mom! Plus, forks and spoons are highly overrated in a wilderness situation and tend to mean more food on the ground for the local rodents to clean up.

Make the Dark Fun

If you have younger children, night in the forest might be nightmare material. You'll want to skip the scary stories with any little ones who tend to get freaked out by Disney movies and keep things lighthearted toward dark.

Break out the glow sticks after dark or hand each child their very own mini flashlight. They'll feel more in control when they have their own light.

If a child is frightened of the noises in the woods, you can turn it into a game. Make up a funny story about an owl who is singing a wakeup song to her babies or tell your children all about the wolf who is trying to impress a loon out on the lake. Kids might still be nervous, but they will be considerably calmer if you make light of the situation.

Don't Let These Things Ruin Your Camping Trip

Even if you spend days planning your trip and ensuring that all your equipment is in order, things can go terribly wrong. Fortunately, most of these situations are predictable if you are an experienced camper, so this list will help you handle your first trip like a pro.

1. Equipment issues. Imagine that it's getting dark and you are scrambling to put your tent together as the sun sets lower and lower . . . only to discover that you forgot the stakes! This scenario happens to first campers all the time. Forgetting an essential piece of equipment is just one issue. Sometimes, it's all but impossible to assemble your equipment even if you have all the pieces and the instructions.

Take the time to try putting up your tent or assembling your stove before you go anywhere. This trial run will help you figure out what works and what doesn't when it doesn't mean the difference between sleeping in the car or having a comfy air mattress.

2. Bugs. The best planned camping trip can go horribly awry if there are swarms of bugs preventing you from even stepping outside your tent. Mosquitoes, flies and sand fleas are all unpleasant and can end up driving you crazy on your camping trip.

Prevention is your best bet in this case. Keep your tent zipped unless you are coming or going to prevent bugs from getting in. Clean the campsite after each meal to ensure there is nothing to draw insects and pay attention to personal hygiene, too. You should also suss out the campsite before setting up and avoid anywhere near stagnant water, since mosquitoes breed in these areas.

Wearing bug spray will help prevent bites, though some people prefer to opt for more natural sprays. You can also light citronella candles or torches around the campsite to help fend off the biters.

3. Blisters. A common mistake on first camping trips is buying all new equipment. The tent is probably fine if new (though it's a great idea to test it first), but things like boots and shoes should never be worn for the first time in the wild. Break any new footwear in before you even think about heading out on a hike. Even if you have well-worn shoes, but haven't spent much time walking lately, you'll want to carry bandages or moleskin with you.

4. Bad neighbors. Established campsites are great for beginners, but they can be awful if you end up with bad neighbors. Look for a campground that has plenty of space between campsites and don't be afraid to ask if you can move if you need to.

5. Rain. Being wet and miserable is probably not your idea of fun. Rain can be rather unpleasant, particularly if you had hiking and other outdoor activities planned. Rain is even more unpleasant if you have equipment issues as mentioned above. To avoid problems, check the weather forecast ahead of time. If it's too bad, you may have to pack up and head home, but first, find out if there are any indoor activities in the area that you can enjoy.

6. Wildlife. You might be in a bear-free zone, but these big predators aren't the only critter that can be annoying when you're sleeping out. Raccoons, possums and other creatures can be pretty annoying, too. Keep your campsite nice and tidy and don't leave food or garbage lying around to attract animals. Avoid keeping food in your tent, as well. This is actually good advice for any location, since bears will sniff out snacks in your tent easily. Most animals are afraid of fire and having a campfire can keep them away while you are awake. Don't leave a fire unattended, though.

7. Fire bans. What's the fun in camping if you can't have a campfire? Check the fire hazard levels in the area you plan to camp in before you go. If there's a ban, you will need to plan around it. A fire ban means no open fires, so check that you're allowed a camp stove before packing one. You have a few other options, though, including an LED or solar lantern for everyone to gather around.

8. Sunburn. Nothing ruins a vacation faster than a nasty sunburn. Apart from using sunscreen and avoiding spending too much time in direct sunlight, you should carry something to help in case these methods fail. A cream with aloe vera in it is a good choice and there are a number of after-burn products on the market, as well.

9. Wet wood. Bring along some dry wood if it has been damp in the area. While it is possible to find dry wood in the forest, life will be infinitely simpler if you have dry wood with you.

10. Swimmer's itch. Staying near a lake? Watch out for swimmer's itch! This unpleasant skin rash is caused by minute parasites in the water that burrow into your skin and die. While the rash is harmless and will go away in a few days, it is quite uncomfortable.

Rinse off after swimming and stick to deeper water when possible to prevent this common problem.

On the plus side, if any of these things do occur during your adventure, they will be the stories you share for years to come!

Conclusion

It doesn't matter how old or young you are, camping can be a great experience. Like anything, there are things that can go wrong, but with a little planning, even the hiccups will be a fun story to tell.

The first time you sleep out in a tent or cook your dinner over a campfire, you'll realize why so many people make this a habit. The outdoors is a place to relax, away from the hectic lifestyles we lead. Even if it's just for a day or two, this can be a terrific way to reconnect with yourself, your family and nature.

Camping is also a terrific idea for kids! Most kids these days don't get nearly as much outdoor time as they should and camping trips allow them the freedom that just isn't possible in the city or even the suburbs. It's also a chance for the kids to learn more about the world around them. Everyone should know how to put up a tent and start a fire and this is the perfect opportunity for your little ones to pick up these skills.

On top of all that, camping with your family is bonding time. Nothing brings everyone together like sitting around a campfire at night, sipping apple cider. Or huddling under a tarp in the pouring rain!

Go camping. You won't regret it.

Made in the USA
Middletown, DE
22 August 2021